Circle of Life
Growing Things

Written and illustrated by Carolyn Scrace
Created and designed by David Salariya

W
FRANKLIN WATTS
LONDON•SYDNEY

Contents

Introduction

To help them grow, plants use
energy from the sun, minerals
from the soil, and water from rain.

In this book you see how
a small black and purple
bean seed grows.
Flowers appear first
and then green beans
that you can eat.

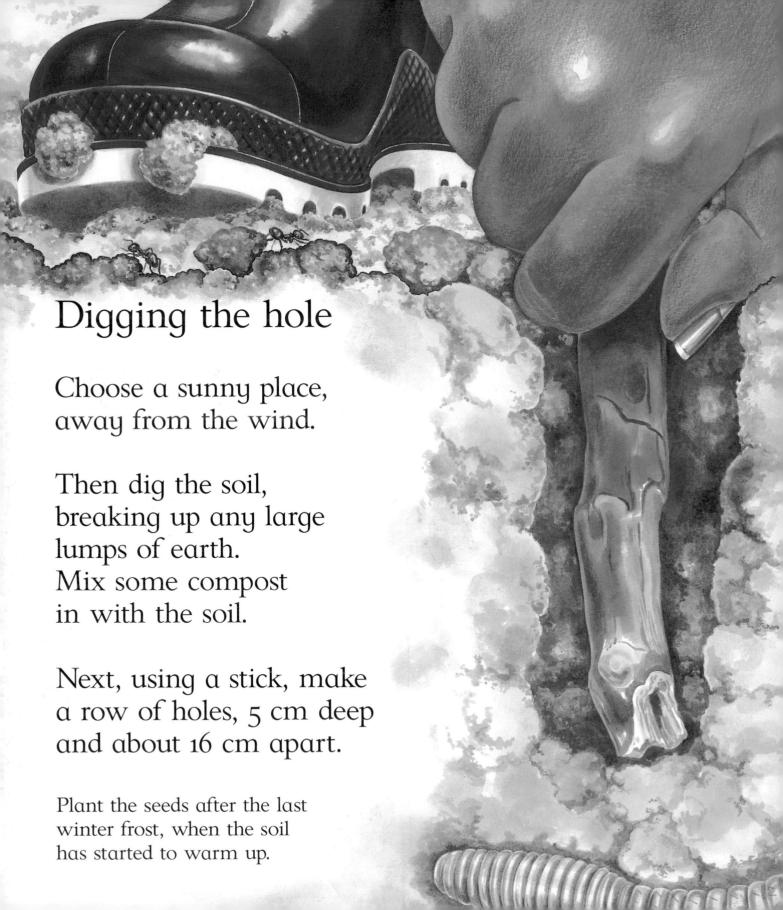

Digging the hole

Choose a sunny place,
away from the wind.

Then dig the soil,
breaking up any large
lumps of earth.
Mix some compost
in with the soil.

Next, using a stick, make
a row of holes, 5 cm deep
and about 16 cm apart.

Plant the seeds after the last
winter frost, when the soil
has started to warm up.

Earthworm

9

Seed

Snail

Earthworm

Planting the seed

Gently push one black
and purple bean seed
into each hole.

Cover it up with
1-2 cm of soil.

Then water the seeds.

Frost will make the
leaves turn black and
the plant will die.

11

Germination

In the warm, damp soil the seed begins to grow.

This is called germination.

First a tiny root sprouts out of the seed coat and grows down into the soil.

Then a shoot grows out and up through the soil towards the light.

Shoot

Root

Slug's eggs

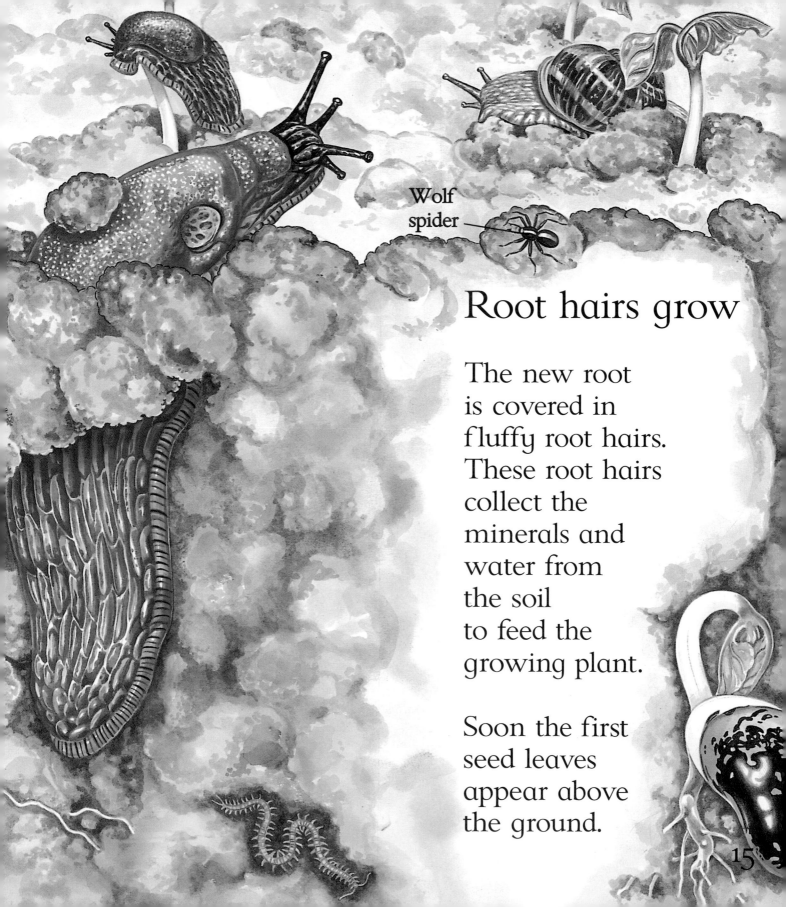

Wolf
spider

Root hairs grow

The new root
is covered in
fluffy root hairs.
These root hairs
collect the
minerals and
water from
the soil
to feed the
growing plant.

Soon the first
seed leaves
appear above
the ground.

15

The leaves grow

The young bean plant grows quickly. Its green leaves use sunlight, air and water to make food.

Below ground, more roots grow, taking in minerals, other nutrients and water from the soil.

When the plants are a few centimetres high, put in 2-m canes for the beans to grow up. Push the canes into the ground 30 cm apart, close to the plants. Cross the canes over at the top and tie them tightly together.

Cane

Field vole

16

17

Magpie

Growing up the cane

The tallest shoot waves slowly about until it finds the cane. Then it begins to wind itself around the cane as it continues to grow.

In hot, dry weather keep the bean plants well watered. Green beans grow anti-clockwise around their canes.

19

Ladybird

The flowers grow

When the bean plants
are tall and strong,
the first flower buds grow.

Aphids feed on bean plants
by sucking out the sap from
the plant stems. Aphids make
honeydew from the sap.
Ants collect the sweet honeydew
from the aphids.
Ladybirds eat aphids.

Flower
buds

Ant

Aphids

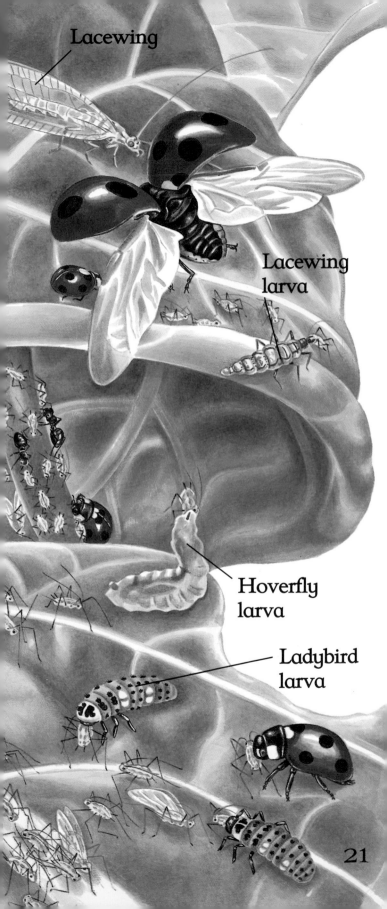

Lacewing

Lacewing larva

Hoverfly larva

Ladybird larva

21

Hoverfly

Pollination

Bees fly from one plant to another. They crawl inside the flowers looking for nectar and their hairy body gets covered in pollen.

When they go to the next plant, some of the pollen from the first flower gets rubbed off onto the next flower, fertilising it.

This is called pollination.

Bee

Shield bug

23

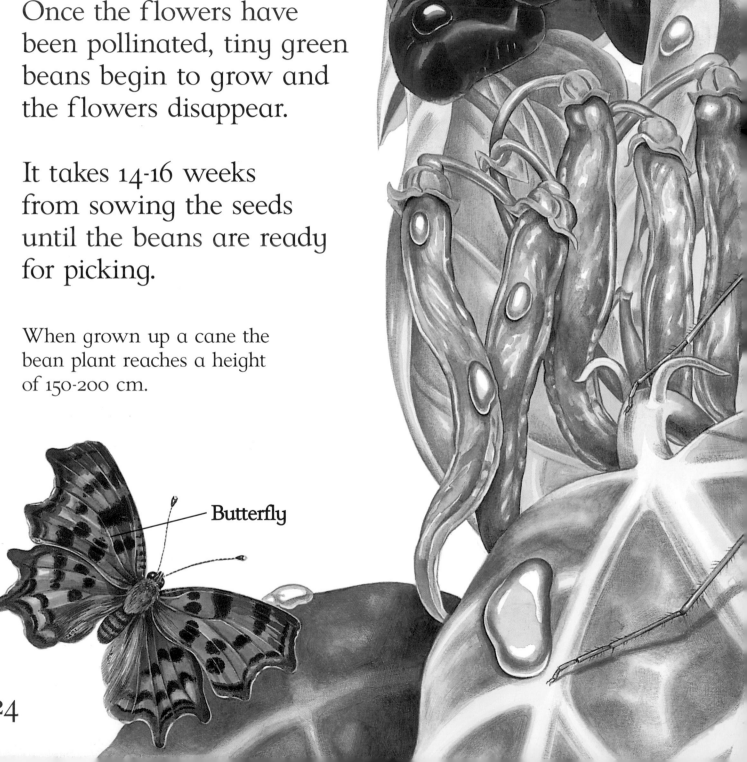

The beans grow

Once the flowers have been pollinated, tiny green beans begin to grow and the flowers disappear.

It takes 14-16 weeks from sowing the seeds until the beans are ready for picking.

When grown up a cane the bean plant reaches a height of 150-200 cm.

Butterfly

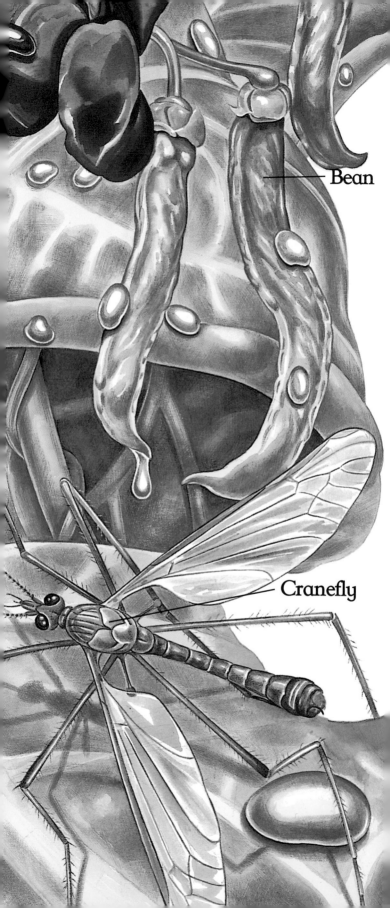

Bean

Cranefly

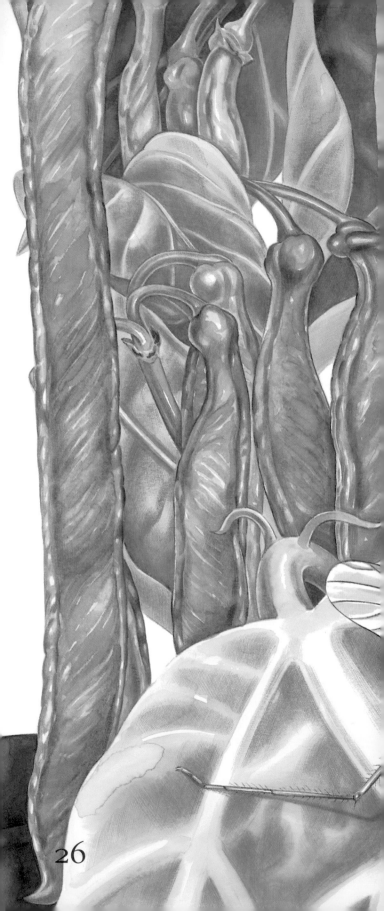

Bush
cricket

Picking the beans

The best time to pick the
beans for eating is when
they are 20-30 cm long.

Keep picking the beans
as they are ready to eat.
The plant will continue
to flower and grow
more beans.

If you leave the
beans too long
they become very
tough and not as
good to eat.

27

The bean plant's cycle

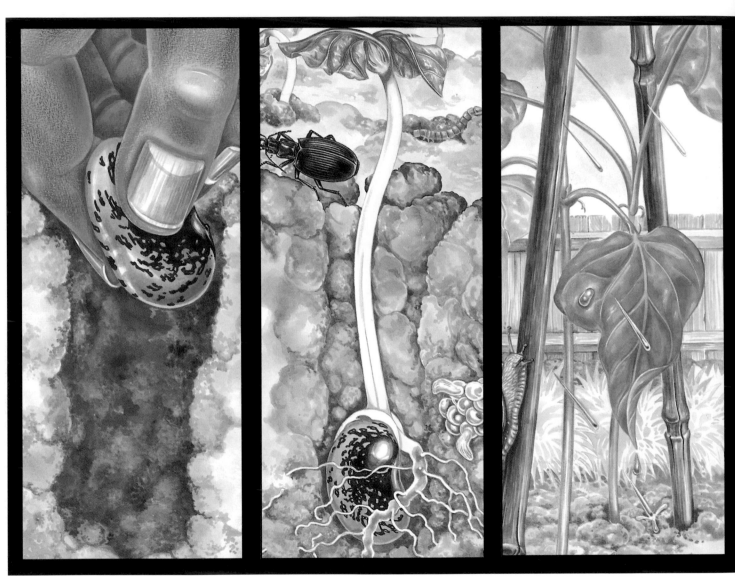

The black and purple bean seed is sown in late spring.

Two weeks later, the young shoot has grown up through the soil. The first seed leaves appear.

After four weeks the bean plant is 40 cm high. After 10 weeks, the plant is fully grown at 1.5 to 2 m high.

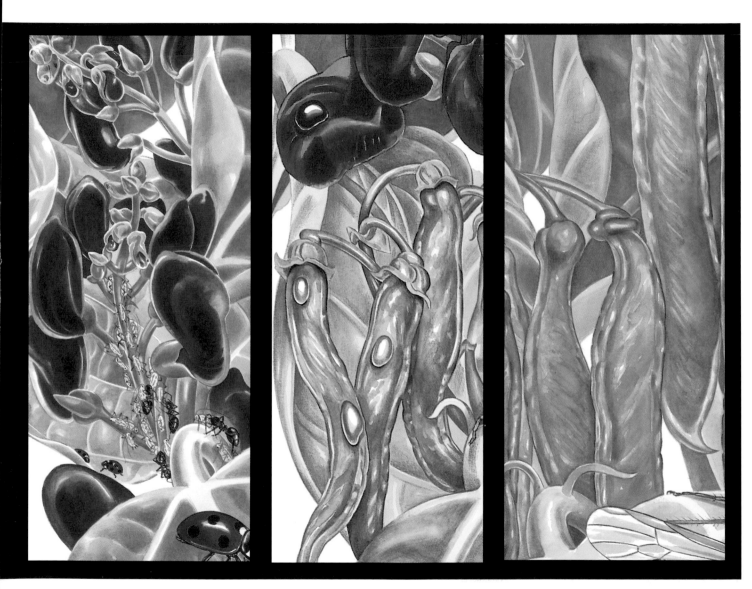

The plant starts to grow flower buds after 11 weeks.

After 13 weeks, the first beans begin to grow.

Between 14 and 16 weeks after sowing the seed, the beans are 30 cm long and ready to be picked.

Growing Things words

Aphid
An insect with a soft oval body, a small head, eyes, two long antennae and a sharp beak.

Bee
An insect covered in stiff black and yellow hairs. It has a sting which it uses in defence.

Compost
Plants that have rotted, and become food for growing plants.

Fertilisation
When the pollen from the male part of a flower joins the female part of a flower.

Germination
When the seed comes to life and begins to grow.

Honeydew
The sweet, sticky fluid that an aphid produces after it has fed on sap.

Ladybird
A type of beetle. It has a small black head, two eyes and two short antennae.

Larva
A stage in the lifecycle of an insect before it grows into an adult.

Minerals
Special food found in the soil. Minerals help plants to grow.

Nectar
Sweet sticky syrup made by flowers.

Nutrients
The parts of food that help the seed or plant to grow.

Pod
The long thin case that holds the seeds.

Pollen
The yellow dust from a male flower.

Pollination
When pollen is carried from the male flower to the female flower.

Root hairs
The tiny hairs that grow out from the roots.

Sap
The watery juice found inside plants.

Seed coat
The thick outer layer of a seed.

Seed leaves
The first leaves that a plant grows from its seed.

Sowing
When seeds are put into the soil, ready to grow.

Index

Language Consultant:
Betty Root

Natural History Consultant:
Dr Gerald Legg

Editors:
Karen Barker Smith
Stephanie Cole

ISBN 0 7496 4427 3

This edition first published in 2005 by
Franklin Watts, 96 Leonard Street,
London EC2A 4XD

Franklin Watts Australia
45-51 Huntley Street, Alexandria, NSW 2015

Created, designed and produced by
The Salariya Book Company Ltd
Book House,
25 Marlborough Place,
Brighton BN1 1UB

Visit the Salariya Book Company at
www.salariya.com

A CIP catalogue record for this book is available
from the British Library.

Printed in Hong Kong